TOOLS FOR CAREGIVERS

- **F&P LEVEL:** B
- **WORD COUNT:** 31
- **CURRICULUM CONNECTIONS:** senses, sounds

Skills to Teach

- **HIGH-FREQUENCY WORDS:** a, I, my, with
- **CONTENT WORDS:** bark, bird, cars, crash, dog, ears, friends, hear, honk, laugh, sing, sounds, waves
- **PUNCTUATION:** periods
- **WORD STUDY:** /k/, spelled k (honk); long /e/, spelled ea (ears, hear); /ow/, spelled ou (sounds)
- **TEXT TYPE:** information report

Before Reading Activities

- Read the title and give a simple statement of the main idea.
- Have students "walk" through the book and talk about what they see in the pictures.
- Introduce new vocabulary by having students predict the first letter and locate the word in the text.
- Discuss any unfamiliar concepts that are in the text.

After Reading Activities

We hear many sounds each day. What sounds do you hear around you at school? Do you hear different sounds at home or outside? Make a list of the sounds you hear and what makes them. What sounds can you make and hear?

Tadpole Books are published by Jump!, 5357 Penn Avenue South, Minneapolis, MN 55419, www.jumplibrary.com

Copyright ©2023 Jump. International copyright reserved in all countries. No part of this book may be reproduced in any form without written permission from the publisher.

Editor: Jenna Gleisner **Designer:** Emma Bersie

Photo Credits: Anatoliy Karlyuk/Shutterstock, cover; Photo Melon/Shutterstock, 1; ABO PHOTOGRAPHY/Shutterstock, 2tl, 8–9; EpicStockMedia/Shutterstock, 2tr, 12–13; wavebreakmedia/Shutterstock, 2ml, 2bl, 4–5, 14–15; Hairem/Shutterstock, 2mr, 10–11; clickit/Shutterstock, 2br, 6–7; PeopleImages/iStock, 3; stockphoto-graf/Shutterstock, 16tl; Utekhina Anna/Shutterstock, 16tr; Svietlieisha Olena/Shutterstock, 16bl; Africa Studio/Shutterstock, 16br.

Library of Congress Cataloging-in-Publication Data
Names: Nilsen, Genevieve, author.
Title: Hear / by Genevieve Nilsen.
Description: Minneapolis, MN: Jump!, Inc., (2023)
Series: My senses | Includes index.
Audience: Ages 3–6
Identifiers: LCCN 2022011556 (print)
LCCN 2022011557 (ebook)
ISBN 9798885240864 (hardcover)
ISBN 9798885240871 (paperback)
ISBN 9798885240888 (ebook)
Subjects: LCSH: Hearing—Juvenile literature.
Classification: LCC QP462.2 .N55 2023 (print) | LCC QP462.2 (ebook) | DDC 612.8/5—dc23/eng/20220321
LC record available at https://lccn.loc.gov/2022011556
LC ebook record available at https://lccn.loc.gov/2022011557

MY SENSES

HEAR

by Genevieve Nilsen

TABLE OF CONTENTS

Words to Know	2
Hear	3
Let's Review!	16
Index	16

WORDS TO KNOW

bark

crash

hear

honk

laugh

sing

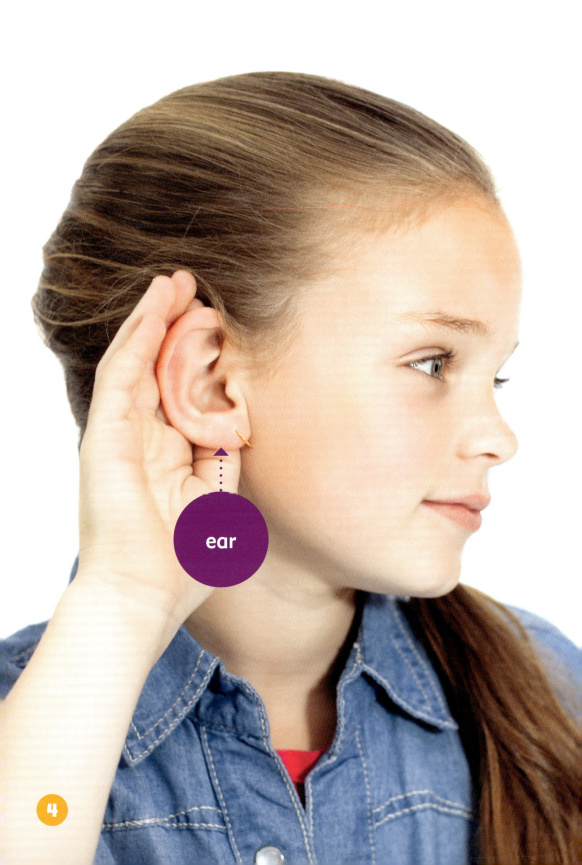

I hear with my ears.

I hear a bird sing.

I hear a dog bark.

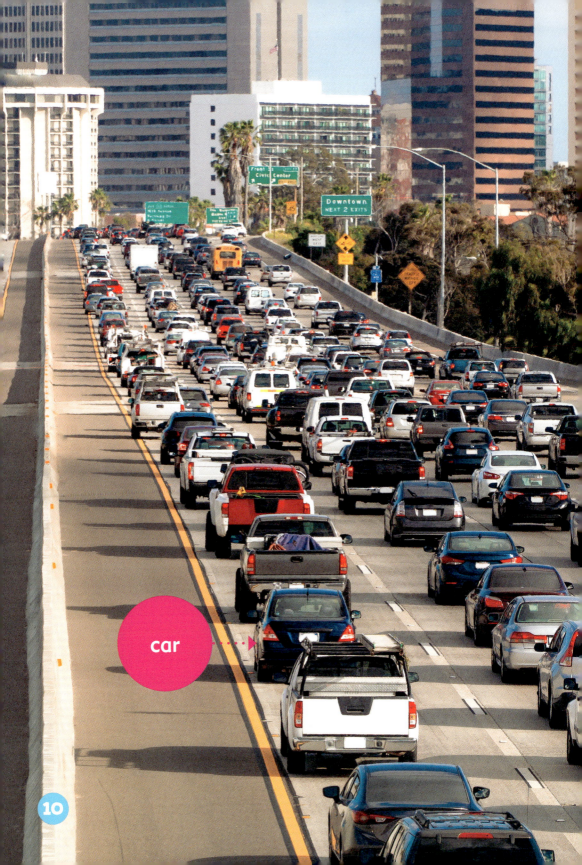

I hear cars honk.

I hear waves crash.

I hear friends laugh.

LET'S REVIEW!

We hear sounds with our ears. What sounds do these things make?

INDEX

bark 9
crash 13
ears 5
hear 3, 5, 7, 9, 11, 13, 15

honk 11
laugh 15
sing 7
sounds 3